# The Panda Bus

# School Bus Stories

By

Bob Parsons

Bob Parsons

Dedication

*Marilyn Lou Brown-Parsons*

Enabler of my writing addiction.

The incidents portrayed in this book are substantially true, but the names and some elements of identification have been changed to protect privacy.

No part of this book may be reproduced or transmitted in any form or by any means, electronic or mechanical, including photocopying, recording, or by any information storage and retrieval system, without permission in writing from the author.



ISBN: 9798458102544

## Praise for The Panda Bus...

The Panda Bus will give a glimpse of the job of a school bus driver.  Funny, insightful, and well written from the perspective of a seasoned school bus driver, Bob Parsons gives just a peak into what it's like to transport the world's most precious cargo – children.

*Vicky Rowald, Retired School Bus Driver 34 years.*
*Retired Assistant Director of Transportation.*

Mr. Bob has hit the nail on the head.  Anybody who has driven a school bus can relate to the stories in this book.  I loved Tony, Tia, and the Girl from Ipanema.

*Keith Young spent 43 years in the school transportation business, as a Driver, a Route Scheduler, Dispatcher, and retired as Supervisor of School Bus Operations in the Austin ISD.  After retirement, he went back to driving for the Round Rock, ISD for 10 years.*

Bob Parsons has always been good at telling stories.  He's even better at living them.  These poignant stories of life on a school bus will make you laugh, think, and yes, maybe cry a little bit.

*The Rev. John Robert McFarland, United Methodist Pastor and Author: <u>Now That I Have Cancer, I Am Whole</u>, <u>An Ordinary Man</u>, and <u>The Strange Calling</u>.*

Bob Parsons

I am loving, loving, loving, your book. So very impressive. I will be sharing it in my in-service training.

*Mike Link Former director of Orchestra, District team leader and department chair of choir at McKinney Boyd High School. Director of music and worship, Aldersgate United Methodist Church, Carrollton, Texas.*

# Table of Contents

# Preface

Some of my fondest memories, of the years I drove a school bus, were made sitting around a table in the bus drivers' lounge hearing and telling stories.

One day during Halloween season (starts in mid-October in Texas), one of my driver friends came into the lounge, laughing. "I had the funniest thing happen today on my elementary run", he said. "I have these two little pre-school girls that sit right behind me, and they got into a conversation about what their mothers called them. They mentioned a bunch of the cute names their parents called them, like cutie pie, honey child, baby, darling, and such. Then one of them said, "My mommy calls me, her little dumpling". For some reason, they found that funny and started giggling and bouncing around in their seats. They added nonsense adjectives to the dumplin'. "You're a window dumplin'...giggle, giggle. "You're a water bottle dumplin' ...giggle, giggle, while falling out of their seat. It calmed down for a minute, after I gave them a cool-it look, in the rear-view mirror. But it started up again when I stopped to pick up a student. They saw a bunch of Halloween pumpkins, in the front yard. That set them off, again. You're a Pumpkin Dumplin. Pumpkin Dumplin. Pumpkin Dumplin. Shouting, bouncing, pointing their chubby fingers at each other. Saliva was coming out of their mouths. I had to stop the bus and calm them down. "It was so funny", my driver friend said. Laughing, he sat down. We all stared at him.

Such stories are fond memories to me, but more importantly, I think such stories remind people of the things that happened in their lives. Who has not been thrilled at the antics of little girls? You may have never driven a school bus, or even ridden one, yet stories that come out of them are familiar in almost any setting. The Panda is parable.

One afternoon, while driving a bunch of high school students, home, they began to sing the Beatles' song, "We all live on a yellow submarine, yellow submarine, yellow submarine." We all live in a yellow school bus.

The question must arise, as to the truth of the stories presented. The answer is "pretty much". They may or may not be exactly true, and certainly they are not accurate in time, place, and personal names. On the other hand, it is true, that I drove a school bus, for fourteen years for the Round Rock, Texas ISD, and a couple years, long ago, for the Schulenburg, ISD. I did experience things upon which these stories are based, enhanced, a bit, for dramatic effect.

Being a preacher, I could not restrain myself from writing commentaries on the stories. Ignore the commentaries if you like. The most important thing is the stories and what are for you. Readers should not be distracted by my rhetoric...no matter how smart I think I am in telling you what they mean.

I hope my stories may be as enjoyable and helpful to you, as the stories shared with me by my fellow bus drivers, were to me. The stories are best read as art forms, open to interpretation by the reader. However, if you desire more context and interpretations to the stories, you will find it in the Epilogue.

# Chapter One

*Courage*

*The Irrepressible Mark Kildare and the Like*

Before he rode the Panda, I had met Mark. With a broad smile and warm eyes directed toward me, he accompanied his mother and two sisters to the bus stop every morning to see his older siblings off to school. Back then, Mark toddled along with the help of heavy leg braces and a firm mother's hand on the back of his collar. Crutches were not an option for him because his slender arms were too frail support his weight. They were fused at the elbows in a permanent V shape leaving the impression he was giving a double arm wave or signaling someone had just scored a touchdown. Every morning, I looked forward to seeing him standing down at the foot of my stairwell with an energetic "Good morning, Mr. Bob".

After seeing him every school day for a year, I did not see him again for two years. I missed him. He was off to preschool and kindergarten on a special-needs bus. So, what a wonderful surprise to see him on his first day as a first grader. There it was...the same smiley face at the foot of the stairs and the same warm "Good morning, Mr. Bob". The arms were still in a stiff V, but the leg braces were gone, and mother was no longer holding him up by his collar. He climbed up the stairs one waddling step at time. Swinging his body from side to side, he motored down the aisle and sat beside a neighborhood friend. All accomplished with a pack on his back and a bouquet of flowers for his soon-to-be teacher.

There is a strict rule on every bus that students are required to enter and exit the bus one step at a time. I mention it to all my riders, and it is written on the top step. I guess Mark did not get the message. On the evening run of that first day, as I stopped at his stop, he walked down the aisle, took one step down into the stairwell and then launched himself off the second step, skipping the ones below. I gasped. My mind raced in expectation of seeing him sprawled face down in the concrete street with his pencil thin legs sprained and broken; his book laden backpack pinning him down. Instead, he landed firmly on his feet and turning to me, with arms raised, he flashed a broader smile than usual, giving me a double thumbs up. His mom was there, and I fully expected a reprimand for my allowing such a dangerous leap. Instead, I got a sidesways glance and shrug of her shoulders that sent a message of surrender, as if to say, "There he goes again, and what can you do." His sisters got off the bus as if nothing new had happened. What are you going to do with a little boy who is going to live his life pushing the boundaries?

Mark may have been limited in physical dexterity, but his heart was fully functional. I am not a child psychologist, but I speculate that two things had come together in this young boy's life to get him through the pain and frustrations of his physical handicaps-he had more than fifty surgeries in the first six years of his life- and made it possible for him to have a smile on his face, to face the world with friendly disposition and abundant courage. First, he was loved and cared for by devoted parents and two doting, older sisters. In the infant stages of his life, it was not his confidence and mental capacity that set the path for his thriving. It was his family who faced with courage his daily encounters with pain, provided the numerous rounds of corrective surgery, hung in there through all the setbacks and kept hope alive. Mark was loved and cared for before he was able to love and care for himself...or anyone. He was a lucky boy. But, somewhere along the line, from birth to the mighty leap out of Panda's door, he chose to be a self-confident, happy, and courageous boy, in total disregard of his obvious handicaps.

There is a good reason why I looked forward to seeing Mark. He offered the love and courageous example that enhanced my life. It was not so much of him standing at the bottom of the Panda's door looking up at me, as me looking up to him.

When Mark graduated to middle school, I missed seeing him for a while. Years later, I was assigned to drive a high school swim-team field trip. There he was standing at the bottom of the stairwell, with the compulsory peroxided blonde hair of all swimmers, looking up to me. The same smile, the same "Hi, Mr. Bob. S'up?" His welded arms had been freed and there was more muscle in his legs.  He had gained some height and weight, but he was still much smaller than average. His body had changed, but nothing had changed about his air of confidence.

As he stood there and as we exchanged greetings and memories a picture came into my head, of Michael Angelo's David. My wife and I had seen his statue of David, the Old Testament and Torah hero of Israel, stands in a museum in Florence, Italy. I am certain that there are many interpretations of what Angelo desired to convey in his marvelous sculpture, but to me the message is clear. The look in David's eyes and the sturdiness of his stance says, "Come and get it". Familiar to the biblical story, I know the evil the youthful David was addressing was the terrifying giant, Goliath. Regardless of the physical danger in facing an armored and weaponized giant, David armed with three stones and a slingshot, stands in a loin cloth, his gaze filled with intensity and determination.

The face I saw in the gallery of the Florence Museum was the same face looking up at me from Panda's stairwell—the David look. Mark's body bore little resemblance to that of Angelo's magnificent young man, but the look and posture were the same. As inspiring as Angelo's homage to human courage was, it could not compare to that of this young man, standing before me in the flesh. It is a wonderful blessing to have young boys and girls, who have faced hardship beyond our knowing in our lucky lives, and have not only survived, but by the nature of their choices have come out stronger, more confident, more courageous, and happier than all who stand around them.  I sometimes wonder if I would have been a school bus driver if I did not get paid for it.  If every child was Mark, I certainly would.

# Chapter Two

*Discipline*

*Connie and Carl: Too Much and Too Little*

Talk to someone who is not a school bus driver, and they will tell you they do not want to be a school bus driver because of the kids. They are not afraid of driving a forty-five-foot yellow truck. They just do not want to drive one loaded with a bunch of children. They would be right to be wary. Driving a school bus is relatively easy once you have gone through drivers' training. Fill the seats with children and things get a bit dicey. Suddenly, the situation demands additional skills. School bus driving involves situations that call for some expertise in child/adolescent psychology, conflict management, institution systematics, diversity training, sexual harassment training, record keeping, intercom communications (ten four to that), map reading, elementary diesel engine mechanics ("I think that doodad that is connected to the whatcha-ma-call-it is g-broke), contemporary music appreciation, litigation law, and cleaning up vomit. To name a few.

Of course, no one has all those abilities. Absent qualification training in all the above situations, a good school bus driver's most significant skill set is the ability to handle surprises.

"Mr. Bob, Eddy just threw up on my backpack."

"Mr. Bob, Tommy's nose is bleeding."

"Oh, how cute, you can actually suck the snot out of your nose directly into your mouth."

Sometimes, the surprises are not limited to the interior of the bus. "Hello, Transportation East, I have a couple parents fighting over custody of Janet. Oh No, he just pushed her. She slapped him. They are yanking on Janet..."

Sometimes, the issue may not be outside the bus, or in the bus, but the bus. "Transportation. This is the Panda bus. Would you call the fire department, please? My dashboard is on fire."

Thank goodness, most transportation departments do provide training and workshops on many of the surprises that a driver may confront...including the use of the hurl kit for cleaning up up-chuck. (Of all the devices of modern innovation, the material that turns liquid body excretions into dry, scentless granules is at the top of my useful list, just after air conditioning.)

Sexual harassment and diversity training is mandated and well-covered by special presentations and spelled out in the Drivers' Manual. The Drivers' Manual was required reading in the district in which I worked. We had to sign a paper saying we had read it. The Manual covers a great deal of information that helps drivers avoid running into unexpected situations, like running into unexpected mailboxes. Most of the items of instruction began with the words "Do Not". There was a whole section on how to use your mirrors. Another on the ten-point safety check of the bus before you start the engine-or was it twelve points? There is a section with about twenty, single spaced pages listing ten thousand violations with demerit points allotted in measure of the seriousness of any said violation. Not just driving violations, but things that you must not do in regard the cleanliness of the bus, relationships to riders, parents, staff, peers, teachers, mechanics, and administrators. Regarding mechanics, *"Drivers are not allowed to address mechanics directly to report a problem on your bus. All requests for maintenance must be written up on the appropriate request form and placed in the shop office drop box provided."* (Where they will die and be buried in the grease well in about two weeks. That last comment is not meant to be critical of bus mechanics. Some of my best friends are bus mechanics. The school district served one of the fasting areas in the nation. Sometimes, things do not get done in a timely fashion, because there were never enough mechanics or bus drivers to cover the growth. Frequently, mechanics were pulled off their duties to drive a bus.)

Another section was devoted to measures of physical fitness, like being able to pick up at least fifty pounds and drag it thirty feet. A requirement, I suppose, of helping drag unconscious kindergarteners of the bus.

The point of all this verbosity, on the value of training sessions and reading the Manual, is to say, you could attend every training session under the sun and memorize the Manual, and that would not complete the knowledge required to handle surprises. Worse yet, even with all that book learning, years of experience and listening to all the stories in the lounge, you will still be confronted with unheard of surprises, that require your handling. In those "gotcha" moments, I believe most common-sense bus drivers will find a workable solution if they pay heed to two broad rules for guidance... (1) never overreact and (2) never ignore. The stories that follow are about two bus drivers...one overreacted and the other did nothing.

### *Story 1: Connie Johnson and the Butterfinger Bar*

There was something a little off about Connie. First, she was not a particularly good driver. She was always on the cuff of being let go because of banging up her bus in minor accidents or gaining minor traffic violations. According to the Manual, ten points for accidents are as many as you can rack up in a school year, before you get fired. Points, like demerits, were awarded based on the seriousness of driving infractions. Scratching a fender in the parking lot got you one point. Ripping off a crossover mirror was two. Causing a wreck could get you anywhere from three to the dreaded ten. Failure to stop at a railroad crossing was a big no-no. One of those and you were gone.

Connie squeaked through most years running on eights and nines driving violation points. But an absence of driving skills was not her only problem. Her bigger problem was discipline. In the end it was not ten points in driving violations that got her let go...it was a how she handled a bit of disorder on her middle-school route.

One hot Friday afternoon while taking her middle-schoolers home, things got a little out of hand, on her bus. Students were throwing things. No one knew at the time what transpired. It was before we had cameras on our buses. I suspect it began, as things are prone to begin on hot Friday afternoons, with a few rowdy students having a bit too much fun. Paper wads can escalate to broken pencil stubs, paper clips and other little weaponry. On this afternoon, the other small projectiles readily available were mini candy bars provided by the middle-school band director, to each of his students every Friday. It is a nice gesture for his students, but not so much for a bus driver.

From what we could hear on our bus radio, rumor, eye-witness accounts, and revelations by Connie herself in the bus drivers' lounge, it was possible to piece a story of what happened. Connie said that she had yelled at the kids to stop throwing things, but they would not obey her. Well, of course they did not. (The first sign of failure in the over-reaction method (ORM) of school bus discipline is the use of yelling. As a rule, I avoid stating absolutes about anything, but gained from my years of hauling students, I know yelling NEVER works. Yelling, like cheer leading, excites the crowd, but in a crowded bus, seldom in positive way.)

The final straw for Connie was getting hit in the back of the head with a mini bar. Hot, tired, and I suspect, upset at herself in not being able to gain control, Connie suddenly stopped her bus in the middle of street and called into transportation and asked the dispatcher to send the police. Back in the old days, our intercom system was on one wavelength, so everyone who had a receiver heard her call for backup.

In most small towns a single deputy would be sent out to investigate. That was not the case in the suburban world, in which Connie drove. In less than five minutes, Connie's bus was surrounded by three patrol cars and two motorcycles, with a half dozen cops asking if anyone was badly hurt in the riot, they assumed, they had been called to quell. Things might have calmed down and Connie's decision to seek law enforcement would have ended on a positive note, if not for the parents of some of the students. A big yellow bus stopped in the middle of the road, surrounded by squad cars draws attention. Several parents, on their separate journeys down the road, saw the action. And of course, every middle schooler on the bus has a cell phone to keep their parents up to date on what is going on. Faster than the coming and going of the cops, the word got out and by the time Connie got her, now very docile group of students on down the road, the parents were waiting at most of her stops, demanding to know what terrible thing had happened on the bus that would bring her to call the law. When they discovered it was all about a candy bar, they were furious. (Note: While it is a bad thing for a school bus driver to overreact, it seems okay for parents to do so.)

Intimidated by the angry parents, Connie once again stopped the bus and called the dispatcher, asking for another set of police to come and put down the mayhem, she assumed was about to cause her bodily harm. In her defense, there are parts of the school district in which it might be dangerous to raise parental ire. Such was not the case in this neighborhood, full of upper middle-class families whose chosen acts of defiance are limited to yelling and complaining to the authorities...some of whom were them. In this case, the dispatcher made a wise move. Instead of calling for police, she sent one of the administrative staff out to the site. I had just finished my run and had some time before my high school route, so the station director radioed me and asked if I would go to Connie's bus to pick up her kids and take them home. Which I did.

Connie was fired, and I was assigned her route, starting on the next Monday morning. I fully expected to encounter a group of out-of-control youth. Nothing could be further from the truth. As the weeks went by, I found that I was blessed to be carrying one of the nicest and most respectful group of youth I had ever known. (That was the beginning of my happy years of driving the same routes with the Panda. Years I called my forty years in the dessert...actually, only ten.)

One might assume they were being nice because Connie's overreaction had frightened them into submission, no matter who their new driver might be. That was not the case. They were just nice kids and understanding parents. If Connie had handled the Friday afternoon breach of conduct without so much drama, they would have been nice for her, also.

In time, I had the opportunity to ask the students what had happened on the famous Friday afternoon. The student who had thrown the mini bar, which hit Connie in the back of head, volunteered he had done it and he was sorry. I thought it was good and brave he had volunteered his mistake and I thanked him for sharing. As he was getting off the bus, I asked him...for no good reason that I can recall...what kind of candy bar it was. He told me it was a Butter Finger. That explained why his buddies called him Butter Finger.

I do not cotton to addressing students with nick names. It seems a bit dismissive. However, in this case I made an exception, as he seemed comfortable with it.

On Friday afternoons, the band director continued to give out mini candy bars. Every band student who got on my bus would rifle through his or her collection of goodies and pick out the Butter Fingers and give them to me. Halloween brought tons of Butter Fingers laid upon my dashboard.

By the end of the year, the saga and fun had subsided. Butter Finger was addressed once again by his real name (Eddie), and we all got on with other matters. As an eight-grader, Eddie went on to a high school and found other ways to get there rather than ride the Panda. However, I would still see him from time to time, as I passed his house on my daily runs. He would exchange greeting and occasionally I would stop the bus and through an open side window ask him, "S'up". One thing that was S'up, was his shiny blue Mustang convertible sitting in his driveway. I enjoyed our quick exchanges, so when Christmas drew near, I decided I would give Eddie a present. I bought the biggest

Butter Finger bar I could find and on the last day before winter break, I laid it on the hood of his Mustang. I left no note. None was required. He would know from whence it came.

Our brief exchanges went on until Eddie graduated and I lost track of him. Then one afternoon, I was stopped at a red light and a young man, with his girlfriend, pulled up beside me. I did not notice his presence, until a Butter Finger flew in my side window and bounced off the dashboard. He smiled and waved and drove away. Now, I smile every time I eat a Butter Finger.

When I was a pastor in San Antonio, I participated in a series of classes, called Citizen Academies, conducted by the public relations officers of the local police department. I do not remember everything I learned about policing in those classes, but I do remember very well the admonition for correct policing, in every situation. It called for officers to never escalate the situation of conflict.

I feel sorry for Connie. Not just because she lost her job, but because she missed out on knowing some exceptionally neat people. I hope the Friday afternoon affair taught her something about discipline. That a bunch of middle school kids are going to throw things from time to time and such behavior is to be expected. It is no big deal. It needs addressing, but in in a manner two degrees in intensity below calling the law.

*Story 2 Carl and the Carling Method*

When driver Carl was terminated no one was surprised. He was famous among us as having the worst controlled bus in the fleet. His disciplinary method, or lack of method became known as "Carling".

Every bus is equipped with a large inside mirror over the front window, by which the driver has an inside view, all the way to the back of the bus. Since most of a driver's time is spent looking forward (hopefully) the inside rear-view mirror is the only way to see what is going on back there. And there is almost always something going on back there.

Carl explained his method in the use of the big, rear-view mirror. He said: "When I started driving, every time I looked in my rearview mirror the kids were all over the place. They were standing up, walking down the aisle, leaning over the seats, facing backwards, hitting each other with their backpacks, and throwing stuff. I tried yelling at them to stop but they would not, so I just stopped looking in my rearview mirror."

The problem with Carling is an obvious disregard for the safety of the students. It is possible to kid oneself there is little danger in standing up in the aisle of a bus while it is moving. If you have never made a sudden stop with your air brakes or by smashing into something solid, it is easy the think nothing bad can happen if the bus is only going 30 mph. Believing that nothing bad can happen at low speed ignores the science of kinetic energy. Mass in motion tends to stay in motion. When a bus, going 30 mph, comes to a sudden stop, in a hundredth of a second, a student standing up continues flying down the aisle at 30 mph until he or she comes to a sudden stop, smashed up against the dashboard or on the pavement, out past the front window. The danger is not limited to the student standing in the aisle. Students sitting backwards or not sitting on their bottoms are also in danger of whip lash, back sprains, concussions and other bone and soft tissue damage. According to *GSU's Hyper Physics Project* a 160 lb. person experiences 30 gs of pressure if wearing a seat belt. That is 2.4 tons of force across the body. If that person is not wearing a seat belt the body experiences 150 gs and 12 tons of force. It is not just the unbelted student moving forward at 30 mph, but all the books, band instruments, and lunch boxes.

From time to time, advisors and peers would talk to Carl about how dangerous it was for his students to go uncontrolled. Supplications to change were ignored with the same Carling, as refusing to look at what was plain to see in his rear-view mirror. Many people gave him advice, "Stop the bus, stand up and confront them face to face." "Write one or two of them up and the rest will get the message." "Get the parents involved." "Ask for a monitor to ride your bus." He ignored it all, deaf to any discussion of his problem, as if the problem would just go away if he did not have to think about it. When called into the office and shown a recording of the behavior of his students, he denied that it was his bus. When shown that the students were his students, he excused their behavior saying the bus was stopped. When shown that the bus was not stopped, because trees were moving past the bus windows, he protested that someone was seeking to destroy his career. The denial turned to sullenness, interrupted by flashes of anger. At that point, Carl was let go.

There seemed to be no hope for him to change his behavior. There may be some mental science truth that doing something that gets you what you want over a long period of time becomes so engrained you become incapable of changing that behavior. As recorded in Jesus' comment in Mark 4:12: *"These people will look and look, but never see, listen and listen, but never hear."*

In his defense, Carling is a method familiar to all bus drivers, especially on hot, Friday afternoon runs, when the children are all hyped up for the weekend augmented by sugary drinks and cake provided by some well-meaning teacher or administrator, as a reward for a good week; or when you are driving back to school with a load of cheer leaders, screaming at the top of their voices and waving their pom-poms out the windows; or in the frantic actions of an ADHD student whose afternoon medication is wearing off. It is on such events, that the little Carl devil appears on your shoulder and whispers into your mind, "Let us just get this over with. Drive the bus and get them home as quick as you can. Ignore them for just this little while." Ignoring a problem is easy to do. All you need to do. Do not look in the mirror.

# Chapter Three

*Peace Making*

*Val and When Violence Comes*

Critical looks are not uncommon. You can get a dirty look if you show up late, or make a wrong turn, or enforce a rule some other driver never does.

Individuals get upset. Singular looks of disappointment happen almost daily. It is a fact...you cannot please everyone. From time to time, you are going to get a look that comes from a slightly turned down face, with squinty eyes peering out from under furrowed brow. I call it the old stink eye.

Sometimes, a whole group of people will grouse at you if you show up late; miss an important turn; or heaven forbid, arrive at the wrong school. I did that once with my high school friends. Absent mindedly, I took them to their old middle school. I got a few "what-an-idiot" looks, but mostly the comments were humorous. "Mr. Bob, is this the high school letting us know we need more work back at the middle school level?" Ha! Ha!

Such looks, whether they come from a group, or some offended individual, can be dealt with by an apology, a word of explanation, capitulation, negotiation, or doing nothing and letting time heal the wound.

Unfortunately, not all dirty looks can be so easily softened, or stink eyes turned to smiles. And so was the case with Val Richardson. He was the exception to the rule. His first look at me was beyond dirty or scowling. It was not squinty eyes framed beneath his brow. It was no "stink eye" to be laughed off. His stare was direct, bold-faced, and hostile. The effect of his look was like a charge of electrons, raising the hair on the back of my neck.

Taken back, I stepped aside and vowed, at the appropriate time, to ask what I had done to raise his ire. In time, I realized there was nothing I had done. There was nothing personal in his rage. I came to know the angry look, the aggressive posturing, the heavy steps, the vulgar language, and the rap music booming from his ear buds had no specific target, nor a particular cause. Val hated teachers, students, the Panda bus, the seats (especially the one I assigned), the tires, the dirt, the trees, the flowers, the bees, the sun, and the moon. I do not know for sure that he hated those latter things, but from what I could see, he had a disdain for everything...all the time. He never let up.

Yet, he was a high school student, and had the right to ride the Panda, as much as anyone else. For a while we (By "we" I mean the other riders and myself) got along. No one challenged him and he seemed content with his bluster. It did not last.

My school district does not allow students to be transported while standing up (as explained above). It was something I had a hard time getting Val to honor. He saw nothing wrong about standing up and walking down the aisle.

One afternoon, before we had moved out of the high school pickup zone, he refused to sit down. From my seat, I politely asked him to sit down. He glared at me and stood his ground. I turned off the engine, set the brakes, and walked to the back of the bus. As I moved down the aisle, Val's half-sister, Alice and his friends, the Sharp brothers, Eddie, and Felix also stood up. Now, I found myself not only facing Val's predictable anger, but the surprise of his being joined in support by three other people.

If there was a chapter in the Bus Drivers Manual on how to handle this situation, it did not come to mind. I could see Alice was not fully dedicated to the confrontation, but the Sharp seemed to be up to it. They offered a legitimate treat. They were both over six feet tall and outweighed me by about a hundred pounds. I could see myself being thrown out the back door. I had a choice to make. I could either continue down the aisle and face their threat or turn around, exit the bus, and seek the help of one of the teachers, standing duty as a bus monitor. I chose to not abandon the bus. I found some hope in disarming the situation in the Sharp brothers. They were members of the same gang as Val, but they had, in the past, been approachable. At times, I had known them to smile, to laugh and kid around. So, I turned my attention from Val to address Eddie, Felix, and Alice...somewhat disarming Val's focus.

Gently and calmly, I offered them a choice. They were free to remain standing if they liked, or they could sit down for the twenty minutes it took to get home. If you chose to remain standing, I told them, I will not be able to move the bus. In addition, if they did not sit down, I would ask a teacher to alert the school cop, stationed nearby. Then, I would make everyone get off the bus. The Law would show up. There would be a big scene. Their parents, or whomever their guardians might be, would be called and they would be upset having to get off work to solve a problem, they had not created. They would not be happy. There would be endless hours of counseling to work out a new Behavior Intervention Program (BIP) or worse, possible assignment to the district's Juvenile Opportunities Center. Plus, a great deal of unknowable bad stuff, over which neither they, nor I would have any control.

Or they could choose to sit down for the twenty-minute ride home, and nothing more would happen. Seemed like and easy choice to me, but I made it clear it was not my choice to make, but theirs. All this explaining of their choice took less time to say than it has taken me to write it. But it was enough time for a crack to develop in their resolve. Alice sat down. The Sharp brothers saw the logic, smiled, and took their seats.

That left me alone with Val. I calmly asked, what he wanted to do. The bus was silent, and I could sense the tension of the other riders. I fully expected Val to remain standing. I sensed that his emotional devotion to rage was so deeply engrained that once it was engaged it would not be something he could control. After a few moments of looking at one another, Val with his hostility, and me with my calm presence (though I was anything but calm, inside), I turned to the side to open a window. Just as I was about to call for a bus monitor, I heard Felix Sharp tell Val to sit down. He sat, and I drove the route without incident. Felix had saved the day, and my buns.

It is in moments like that, your life flashes in front of you. Not your whole life, just those parts related to what is going on right now. The brain is a wonderful instrument when it is hyped on adrenalin. It will draw up pictures of past experiences to inform a solution to the current one, quickly and automatically. (That is why I believe our elders are wiser than we are. They have more pictures to draw on.). And so, as I walked down the aisle to confront Val, a couple picture popped up in my consciousness. One was of the time, years ago when I attended a Civilians Police Academy, mentioned earlier. In my mind's eye, I saw the police instructor saying to never escalate the violence. At the same time a second image arose. In my mind's eye, I could see me grabbing the baseball bat, I used to check tire pressure, and bashing Val over the head with it. As I described above, I chose the former picture over the latter. In the end, it was not me, but Felix Sharp who saved the situation on that afternoon. Still, I was glad I had not grabbed the bat.

Several days went by without incident. In fact, things improved. A kind of trust developed between the four (Alice, Val, Eddie, and Felix) and me. Alice told me they had grown up in the Watts district of Los Angeles. Their mother had been a prostitute and they did not know who their separate fathers were. The had been placed in numerous foster homes and fought over from time to time to be placed back into their mother's care, which never worked out. Alice managed to survive until she was sent by Child Protective Services to live with her mother's mother in Austin. Val refused to leave

Watts. Left on his own, on the street and in the embrace of a gang, Val became a gang banger with a record of juvenile crimes, which got him placed in the care of the California Juvenile Justice System and ultimately, he too, was sent to Texas, to live with his grandmother.

It was obvious to me, why Val was so eternally angry. There was not much in his short life to not be angry about. It certainly was no stretch for me to give him a little slack. As John Bradford the English reformer said, "There but for the grace, God I".

Some rapport developed, as I entered negotiations with the group about playing their iPad rap music too loud and banging out the rhythm with their rings on the metal window frames. I approached them with some choices. They could play their music but not so loudly it could bother my driving. They could keep the beat, but not by pounding on the metal framing. Singing along was okay but had to leave out the mother-f...ing in the lyrics. (Banning the f-word reduced their selection of rap music by 95.5%.). Our interchanges took on a bit of levity. I suggested to them that if they played their rap music from

Monday through Thursday, they should play the music I select on Fridays. To my surprise, they accepted the proposal. I wracked my brain for a week, before bringing them my selection of music. The list included Rod Stewart, Bob Seger, Kenny G, Roy Orbison, Barbra Streisand, and Willie Nelson.

They did not recognize a single artist, much less any of the songs. Their absence of recognition of any of my favorites is understandable. I recognized none of theirs, either. The absence of knowledge, about each other's favorite music highlighted the huge gap in our knowledge of each other's worlds. The experiences we shared, about music, built a little bridge of trust with Alice, Eddie, and Felix. Unfortunately, none of our agreements and conversations, during those happy weeks, involved any consent from Val, who sat through it all in sullen silence.

One morning, Val exited the bus and was standing outside with his friends, as I walked the bus to check for items students might have left behind...a routine occurrence. In the back seat, I found a notebook with Val's name on it. I took it to the stair well and called him over, to retrieve it. He came and for a second, we stood facing one another. Me smiling, with an attempt to be helpful, and him posturing, stone faced and silent.  I dropped the smile and broke the silence asking Val if there was anyone in his life he liked.  To my surprise, he heard me. With an almost normal look on his face, he said he liked his grandmother, the woman with whom he and his half-sister had come to stay, in Texas. For a moment, I had broken through his shell and established a bit of calmness in our relationship.

The calm was not to last. It was broken one hot afternoon when I heard Alice screaming from the back of the bus and saw in the rearview mirror, Val was pounding on her, as she lay on the floor kicking and fighting to get him off. I stopped the bus and rushed to the back, where he now stood over Alice. Alice was crying. I helped her up and set her in a seat across the aisle from her brother. I asked her to move over, and sat down beside her, placing myself between her and Val. With me sitting down and Val standing above me, I had placed him in a superior position. Regardless of my vulnerability, I kept a steady gaze on him. Glaring at each other, I waited for him to say or do something. Finally, I said: "Val,

I am not your enemy. I am just your school bus driver."

His response was typical Val: "Go F..k yourself. Leave me alone and go drive your f...king bus."

I said: "I cannot drive the bus if you remain standing."

(Silence)

He remained standing.

(Silence)

I asked: "Val, what is it you want?"

(Silence) Still standing.

"Okay," I said with some reserve. "You can remain standing if you want but you will need to do it behind a seat and not out here in the aisle. Can you do that?" (I hesitated to give up the no-standing rule, but I felt it was the right thing to do at the time. I flattered myself to think good drivers follow the rules and great drivers do what is right. The Panda bus was not the Star Ship Enterprise, but a prime directive for both Capt. Kirk and me was the same. "Do the right thing.")

Val moved out of the aisle and sat on the back seat with his legs tucked under. I checked Alice and she seemed all right. We finished the run without incident.

I wrote up the incident and turned it in to the high school office and to the transportation department. Val never rode the Panda, again. He was transferred to the Opportunities Center, where he could continue his education and receive the kind of personal attention, he needed to prevent him from hurting other students.

After that, I have no idea what happened to him. I hope his feelings for his grandmother might break through the darkness of his rage, or in some small way my time with him will give him a helpful memory picture. Alice, Eddie, and Felix rode the Panda for the rest of the year. The music subsided a bit. No one stood up when the bus was moving. I learned a great deal about rap music. A happy ending came the last day of school as they were exiting the bus. Felix, the oldest member of the trio, shook my hand with the gang's secret handshake. It signaled that I had just become an honorary member of their gang. I did not go to the meetings.

# Chapter Four

## *Playing*

### *Freddie and the Last Word*

Freddie was a sophomore, but already a BMOC (Big Man on Campus). He did not often ride the Panda, because he had no problem hooking rides with older students, especially with girls, delighted to be associated with his popularity.

In my limited experience, I have observed that high school boys, who excel at sports, are particularly popular with the opposite sex. I have not run into many students on the robotic team, or chess club, being swooned over, because they excelled in their field of endeavor. Freddie looked good in a football uniform...or outside of one. He was also on the swim team, and when stripped down to a bikini bathing suit, dripping wet with his bleached hair (a tradition for male, high school swimmers) shining in the early morning sun, he was not just a good-looking boy...he was gorgeous.

Being handsome is a major plus in the rise of high school social status (or anywhere else), but not every handsome boy is a big man on campus. Nerdy boys may be good looking and still miss the mark for adolescent adoration. Nerdy boys are...well...nerdy. So, looking good is important in high school, but it is not everything. Being good looking was not the sole source of Freddie's bigmanship. He was also smart, humble, polite, and funny.

There is a brief time, a week or so, during the end of school when all extracurricular sports end, giving time for the students to concentrate on their final exams. It is then that the buses are packed with jocks--both male and female-- like Freddie, who would normally be out on the practice field. It was during this short time the Panda was graced with the presence of Freddie.

Most of the Panda kids are exceptionally nice kids. They are polite and friendly. Saying "Hello, Mr. Bob" when they get on the bus and "Thank you, Mr. Bob" when they exit. The girls are particularly nice with their "Thank you" delivered in an octave somewhere above high C. I always felt a hint of flirtiness in it but having never been a BMOC how would I know. The guys just said things like "Bye" and "Thanks" as they rushed by. Not Freddie. He would stop, look at me and deliver some cliché salutation, like, "Have a good one", "Keep up the good work", or "You the Man, Mr. Bob". At first, I was caught off guard by his extra attention and could think of no appropriate response. Then after several times of non-response, I answered his "Keep Cool" with "*Ciao*".

He fired back, "Peace, bro".

I responded, "Keep the Faith".

Freddie responded to my response to his response with "Hey, don't let the bastards get you down".

I said, "Keep a stiff upper lip" (That one caused a pause. Freddie may not have ever watched a British war movie).

His singing "Tomorrow" from *Annie,* while standing in a theatric pose outside the door, ended the repartee for the day. But I knew this thing was not over. I know a contest when I see one. This bantering required quick come backs. I was determined to not let some high school sophomore beat me in cliché competition. I lay awake all night dreaming up friendly salutations.

Freddie started it off the next day. Standing beside me, he paused his exit and said, "Be Cool"

Me: "Smooth"

F: "Always"

Me: "Keep the Faith" (a rerun of the day before)

F: "Don't let the bastards get you down" (another rerun. I was beginning to realize that in addition to coming up with new ones, we were going to warm up by repeating the old ones, which would require remembering the sequence as it grew each day.)

Me: "Don't take any wooden nickels" (I decided to opt out of the memory game, because I could not remember yesterday's sequence.)

F: "Don't let them see you cry"

Me: "Keep your eye on the ball"

The banter went on for a few more bars before I gave up, when he threw in an acronym: "LMAO". I think Freddie felt that I had played dirty by throwing in the "Don't take any wooden nickels" -- a saying outside his age range--so he dropped a contemporary "LMAO" on me. What the heck is LMAO?

By this time, the aisle was backing up. Everyone was laughing. Freddie jumped off the top step and waved goodbye. I asked one of the students what LMAO stood for. "Laughing My Ass Off", she said.

"Aha," I said. I had just entered the new age world acrynomia in which my OS (Old School) limitations made the competition untenable. I chose to withdraw.

It was not to be. Now, the whole bus was involved. The simple "Thank you" and "Bye" were gone. Now, everyone was offering some special, well-wishing salutation expecting some clever cliché from me.

Because the high school is an IB (International Baccalaureate) school it has an unusual number of students of foreign nationality, so, it came as no surprise that language borders got crossed. I got a "*Vaya con Dios*," from Jose, to which I responded, "*a su amigo*"; a "*Shalom*" from Benjamin, to which I responded in kind, "*Shalom aleichem.*" (I did not take Hebrew in seminary for nothing.) It was a bit tougher when one of the Pakistani boys offered an "*Allahu Akbar*". He was pleased with a simple English response: "Yes, He is". Karisah, one of the

Indian girls nodded to me and delivered a sweet *"alavida sahaa"*. I had no idea what that meant, so I just nodded back. (She later told me it was Hindi for "Goodbye") From there on, my foreign language lessons had no end. I boned up on foreign language clichés by going online. In Google Translate you can find an unending source of salutations: *Au revoir, Aaijian, Sayonara, Auf Wiedersehen,* and on and on. I used a few, but the fun had run its course, so I gave up and just started nodding my head and saying, "Yeah, yeah, I know." Thankfully, as with most things adolescent, the novelty wore off and we got back to the "goodbyes" and the high pitched "Thank you", common in white girls. Freddie in his gracious way gave no thought to gloating over my defeat in the grand banter war. Mercy runs deep on the Panda.

The few days of having no after school activities came to an end, and Freddie stopped riding the bus. By the beginning of the next Fall semester, he had acquired a car and never rode the bus again. A year or so later, I saw him on campus. Waving, I said, "WYD" and he answered "BFF." I hope so.

Looking back, I smile at the congeniality of Panda's international community. I wish the jovial banter and friendly competition experienced, in that little microcosm of life, were the ways of the whole world. I am happy that there are schools with IB curriculums that draw a broad diversity of students. I was glad the Panda was IB, too.

However, even the jerk-free Panda was not immune to prejudicial outbreaks. Some snobbery can be overlooked, or gently judged with a "Careful you don't drown with your nose stuck up like that." But sometimes biases turn nasty, when the biaser goes too far to hurt a biasee. Janet was an eight grade, middle school cheer leader...pretty, tall, and full of herself. No need for an alarm bell to go off with concerns about her arrogance. That is pretty much the stance of most eight graders regarding all underclass students. Cheer leaders, perhaps, more so than others. There is no need for a bus driver to practice behavior modification. Just wait. (Eighth-grade snobs learn humility the first week of high school.) But Janet took it too far, one afternoon while students were loading my bus. My welcoming riders on board was interrupted by a cat fight in the back of the bus. Janet was attempting to get an Asian girl to go sit up front. What I heard was, "Where you belong". The IB middle school and the Panda, were full of Asian girls and boys, who had been carefully taught that they belonged, like any other student. So, in the end, it was not the Asian-American that was moved, but Janet. Unsupported, by her eight grade friends, Janet stood alone. With a huff, she plopped down in her assigned seat, across the aisle from her Asian friend. I almost cried. Okay, a tear or two of joy.

It seems true, that bigotry requires a group. Prejudices require precedence to maintain itself. When Janet found herself alone in her bias, her confidence was shaken and her snobbery humbled. Way to go Panda bus!

# Chapter Five

*Belonging*

## *The Americanization of Anashya Katimandar*

Anashya and his sister Ishya came with their parents and one set of grandparents from India in November, so they did not begin riding the Panda until the middle of the Fall semester. On the first day of riding the Panda, they were accompanied by their anxious parents and grandparents. Mr. Katimandar wore the Austin techie look of khaki pants, starched white shirt and brown loafers, typical of what you might expect of a tech engineer recently transplanted from India (or California). The mother and grandparents were dressed in traditional Indian clothing. The grandfather in pressed, white kurta pajamas and the women in elegant saris. Both their parents spoke excellent English, so I was able to assure them their children were on the right bus, going to the right school. Anashya, a fifth grader and Ishya, a fourth grader spoke broken English limited to common phrases. I found them seats, near a couple other Indian students, thinking they would be able to share in their native language. It did not work out. Those Indian children did not speak much Hindi, having been born in the United States. Regardless of the strange environment for Anashya and Ishya, they seemed to make it through the first morning without a great deal of anxiety.

Returning them home that first day, I was once again greeted by the whole family, with a crisp "Thank You!" and nothing more. I sensed a bit of coolness in their reception and jumped to the conclusion that there was some form of caste observance going on. Dressed in their fine clothing and living in an up-scale neighborhood, I imagined they saw me as *Dasa*, a mere servant. Or perhaps, they were not being aloof, but simply experiencing some timidity as strangers in a strange land.

The reserve shown by the parents was present in their children. For several weeks neither Anashya nor Ishya greeted me. The relationship I had hoped would make them feel welcome, did not develop. They were as cold to the advances of the other students as to me, including the other Indian kids. Each day, they quietly got on the bus, walked to the back, found their assigned seats, and said not a word. I should have been happy. Silence and obedience on a school bus is golden. However, I was hoping they would fit in.

In this world of diversity, of which the Panda is a perfect metaphor, it is understandable that young boys and girls hold tightly to their tribal traditions. There is security in not fitting in. Social distancing is appropriate when everyone around you has a place, and the only one in your place is you. Worse choices can be made than silent reserve.

I have chosen to limit this story to the adventures of Anashya, in exclusion of his sister, simply because his story is more dramatic. However, the challenges he faced were known equally by Ishya.

When Anashya first rode the Panda, he looked like an English schoolboy. He came on board with his thick black hair well groomed, his feet laced up in leather shoes (no sneakers for him), crisply ironed and creased Khaki pants, starched long sleeved shirt covered with a solid green, woolen vest sweater. He was more Ivy League than Asian. Nothing was out of place, except the full-sized cricket bat. I did not ask him why he brought the bat, but I was certain it was not part of the elementary, athletic program. Maybe, it was for Show-n-Tell. But after a month of hauling, it around, cultural exchange did not seem likely. When January passed into Spring break and we neared the end of the school year, Anashya held tight to the bat, which from time to time he accessorized with a cricket helmet and face mask. The normal response of the kids on the Panda to some unexplained behavior was to demand an explanation. "Hey Susie, What's with the boots?" That question followed by a bad rendition of "These Boots are Made for Walking." However, no one bothered Anashya, and Anashya bothered no one.

For months, nothing changed. Same Anashya. Same bat. Same silence. But nothing stays the same, forever. Finally, Anashya's behavior began to change. Brought on, perhaps, when his sister decided to sit with some fourth-grade girls, leaving Anashya alone. The Panda is a crowded bus. There is not room for anyone to have a seat all to themselves, so another fifth-grade boy took Ishya's place. That boy was Tommy. I gave him the seat beside Anashya because Tommy had worn out his welcome with his former seatmate. Tommy was a bit ADHD and when not medicated (His meds frequently wore off on afternoon runs) he found it hard to control himself...the opposite of Anashya. I did not expect the arrangement to last. What a surprise it was when they began to talk with one another. Since they were sitting, far back in the bus, where fifth-graders reign, I had no idea what they talked about. The bat was seen less often, and the helmet never appeared again. In April, six months after first boarding the Panda, Anashya said "Good Morning, Mr. Bob", for the first time. I almost ran into a mailbox. What began as baby steps in social exchanges, turned into major steps in assimilation. He began to laugh, to tussle with other boys, and even challenged an Alpha male to the back seat of the bus. Horror of horrors, I caught him chewing gum (a major no-no on the Panda). Between April and the end of May (when school is out), the reserved, distant, silent, obedient, Indio-English boy was almost gone. The Khaki pants were replaced by shorts, the laced-up leather shoes by flip-flops, and the cricket bat by a softball, I had to take away from him, because he and Tommy were playing pitch and catch with the third-graders, five rows away.

Anashya was not the only one who changed. Loud and rambunctious Tommy settled down. It seemed that all he wanted was a friend. Finding a buddy in Anashya, his hyperactivity subsided.

Every bus driver longs for a bus full of silent and obedient students. It is a great pleasure to drive when everything is calm and quiet. For that reason, I wondered why I was pleased to see a silent and obedient Indian/English schoolboy turning into a boisterous American kid, like all the other students on the Panda. As the adage goes, "Be careful about what you wish...for you shall surely get it". I was happy to have his aggressiveness, if it meant he was fitting in, and had found a friend in Tommy. I will take belonging over isolation, every chance I can. Belonging is always costly to individuality. I miss the cricket bat.

# Chapter Six

*Understanding*

*Tony, A Lovesick Boy*
Tony looked more mature than his teen age, but he was not. He was in his emotional development precisely where his testosterone level placed him. Growing rapidly with just a bit of acne, he was a handsome boy, but still not a man. Friendly and polite with "Hello, Mr. Bob" on entering the Panda and "Thank you" when he left.

Tia was a pretty exchange student from Estonia. Part of THS' International Baccalaureate (IB) program, which was aggressive in recruiting foreign students. She was shy, soft spoken, and had an air of aloofness about her that added a bit of mystery. She could pass as a *Vogue* cover girl in her dress and mode of moving about. When she entered the bus, everyone noticed. Like the "Girl from Ipanema, "she goes walking and when she passes, each person she passes goes...Ah".

Most of riders of the Panda were drawn to her, but to say that Tony was drawn to her, would be a gross understatement. Do moths love flames?

He went gaga from the moment she first came aboard.

Residing in the mind of every young boy's, is an image of the perfect mate. They clearly imagine the color of hair and eyes, complexion, shape, height, smile, poise…the whole thing. With that vision of the perfect girl planted in their brains, they go shopping, full-time. That is why young boys, and some not-so-young men are enamored by exotic pictures of women, they can find in erotic magazines, and on the internet. They look at girls in pictures, and real-life, in an endless search for a match to perfect picture in their minds. The perfect fit is hard to find. But Tony found his. It was Tia. His fascination was obvious, to everyone. He could not stop looking at her. As she got on the bus, swaying past him down the aisle, he would follow her like a barn owl, nearly twisting his head off. When he finally turned to face the front, I could see that he was stunned, like a deer in the headlights.

Many married couples and significant others claim that their attraction was "love at first sight". And so, it was for Tony. Unfortunately, Tia did not appear to share the attraction. In fact, she hardly noticed him. It would seem reasonable, to those of us of a more mature understanding of human relations, or those who have never been lovesick, to expect at some point, for Tony to make a move on Tia. He did not. Not all lovers flow like "a river to the stream". Buried, deep inside their psyche, is a voice of warning. "Do not go there, you fool. She is way outside your league." They are paralyzed by the fear of rejection. Better to bathe in unspoken adoration, than do anything to bring an end to the slightest hope. The catatonia, of the gaga state, is the consequence of getting stuck in immobility, because of the inner conflict between the one's head and one's heart. It is not uncommon. Thomas Jefferson wrote a booklet on it called, appropriately, "Head and Heart", a dialogic reflection on his passion for a French woman. (The French know this stuff).

Fortunately, love sickness is not terminal (in most cases), nor do its symptoms last forever. Slowly, its victims do begin to make some meaningful advances, if only in small ways. To engage Tia in a conversation was, at this point, still beyond his courage, to attempt. So, like so many other youngsters of the techie generation, he decided he would text her. Not having her cell phone number, he approached me for it.

T: "Mr. Bob, don't you have every student's number?

Me: "I have only their parents' numbers, so I can call them in an emergency."

T: "Can I have Tia's parents' number"

Me: "Her parents live in Estonia." I knew what he wanted but I enjoy torturing students.

T: "The family where she is staying?"

Me: "I cannot give you that number. It's confidential."

T: "Oh. Well thanks anyway."

Stymied by the absence of a phone number to text, it took a month for Tony to finally talk to Tia. I have no idea about what. Before winter break, he had moved across the aisle from her, and was entering into moments of banter with her and her girlfriends. Things were moving along. "This is good," I thought to myself. In my optimistic mind, I imagined a love-at-first-sight story with a happy ending for these to lucky youths. I could see an eighty-year-old, Tony talking about how he loved her at first sight and eighty-year-old Tia, proclaiming how she finally gave in to his persistent wooing. In my mind it was meant to be. Only it was not meant to be. There was a problem of geography. With the term of her exchange coming to an end, Tia went home to Estonia during the winter break.

Because school bus drivers are the first school employees to see the students each morning, they are the ones who sometimes offer the breaking news. As Tony was getting off the bus the first day after Winter Break, he asked, "Where's Tia?" I had to tell him she had gone home to Estonia and would not be coming back. There is an expression of sadness that accompanies the announcement of death...a slumping of posture, a lowering of the head, a deep sigh of sorrow. To witness Tony's reaction to the news of Tia's departure, you would think that I had announced her death. There was, of course, no whimpering, tears, or crying out. It was a display of sadness, shown in silence and somberness. The sunny Tony darkened. His sun set and the black clouds moved in. As Roy Orbison wails, "You won't be seeing rainbows anymore."

People make jokes of lovesickness. We call it puppy love and opine that "they will get over it." We old dudes have forgotten how dangerous young romance can be. The ancient church and social traditions knew it well and built walls between the sexes in the attempt to control the consequences of youthful passions...to no avail. The tragic ending of "Romeo and Juliet" is no comic fantasy. Love hurts. And gaga can kill. Many teenagers have been lost, that way. Love sickness is not restricted to the young. Many in a mid-life crisis have tragically thrown away their stability, moral codes, fortunes, vows and sometimes their last breath, chasing a mate, who matches the sexual idol in their brains.

Tony's grief was serious. I hoped a school counselor, his parents, and Tony's friends were aware of his depression, and its cause. In the brief periods on the twenty-minute rides to and from school, I avoided demeaning his pain, taking seriously his state of mind. We spoke briefly of Tia. He asked me where Estonia was. He shared some of the things she had said and done. In the last weeks before Tony graduated, I congratulated him and asked him what he planned to do for the summer.

"I am thinking about going to work, so I can save enough money to go to Estonia." My first thought was he was kidding, but on second thought, I was not so sure. I said, "I hope it works out for you, Tony."

I wish I had an ending to this story, but of course there is no ending because Tony decided not to end it. And that might be the most important thing to know.

# Chapter Seven

*Caring*

*Lucy Fussbudget*

From time to time, everyone complains about something. However, there are a few people who seem to complain about everything. There is a name for such persons. The *Merriam-Webster Dictionary* defines fussbudgets as people who are *frequent complainers over trifles*. Lucy Morgan Townsend was a fussbudget.

Lucy was a rather small, cute (are not they all), curly blonde-haired, six-year-old first-grader, with the light skin indicative of her parents' Nordic origins. She was the older sister of a pre-school brother, Tommy, who also rode the bus, and a baby brother, back home. As a child born in England to Anglican parents recently stationed in the United States, she spoke with a sharp accent that to my rough East Texas ears sounded condescending. I am sure my interpretation of her over-bearing speech pattern was my prejudicial problem, not hers. After all she was only a first grader. On the other hand, I was not wrong about her being a fussbudget.

I have never done a thorough study of fussbudgetism, nor have I read a scientific thesis on the subject. My wisdom on the topic is grounded in the fact I was born the youngest of four brothers. My three older brothers felt it was their responsibility--being older and wiser--to critique everything I did or did not do. I believe most older siblings are fussy.

In addition to the insights received from years of little-brotherhood, I am well-experienced in identifying fussbudgets through forty years in the pastorate. I am sure other institutions have hyper-critical people in them, but it seems to me religious institutions have more than most. Jesus thought so, too. The New Testament records twenty-five instances of Jesus warning the Scribes and Pharisees (religious leaders) of their hypocrisy. The most familiar recorded in Matthew 7:5, "You hypocrites, first take the log out of your own eye, and then you will see clearly to take the speck out of your brother's eye." Hypocrisy and fussiness go hand in hand.

Fussbudgetry and hypocrisy share the same characteristic because they are both pretentious. Both behaviors are found in persons who pretend to know things better than anyone else. Fussbudgets and hypocrites are, in their minds, know-it-alls who cannot keep their directives to themselves. And thus, they also tend be loud mouths. Like the guy in the restaurant, three tables over who can be heard throughout the establishment explaining some election outcome or scientific process behind nuclear fusion. Of course, in reading over the complaining I have just written, I may have very well gone from valid insight to borderline fussbudgetry, myself. Takes one to know one.

Lucy was not borderline, she was a certified (by me), fully developed fussy person and proud of it. The other children on the bus agreed with me. They responded to her critical attitude by staying as far away from her as possible. Something hard to do on a bus. I had, on occasions, attempted to seat her with more accepting children. Lucy had a better idea, for where she should place herself...immediately behind me.  There, she could oversee my driving and disciplinary skills and provide necessary corrections, right into my ear.

"Mr.Bob, you shouldn't let Eddy stand up while the bus is driving."

That is how she said it. As if she had read the bus driver's manual. "Student must be seated at all times when the bus is moving" *Page 4, Rule # 4.*

"Mr. Bob, the heater is not working."

"Mr. Bob, I hate all this noise. You could make them quiet if you stopped the bus and clapped your hands three times, like Mrs. Thompson does."

"Mr. Bob, you need to keep both hands on the steering wheel." *Page 4, Rule # 14.*

I was impressed she knew so much about driving a school bus. I never said fussbudgets were not smart. She may have very well read the manual. When you are a know-it-all, you need to spend a lot of time reading.

Grapevine Trail is a narrow road that trends along a canyon rim in a hilly, in new up-scale subdivision. The sub-contractors, who did the road work, must have made mistakes laying the base material, because for the entire length of the road it has little rises and dips, like a gentle roller coaster.

Riding on its undulations gave you a funny little thrill and a tickle in the pit of your stomach. The Panda kids loved it. To enhance the fun, they would raise their hands above their heads and give out loud screams of laughter. At times, a few would stand in front of their seats...a behavior I forbid, after Lucy pointed out their infraction. Lucy stayed seated, frowning on the whole thing as disobedient behavior and a major breach in leadership on my part. She told me (I started to write suggested but *told* is accurate) I needed to stop going down Grapevine Trail, and to help me out, she had mapped out an alternate route, that while further was much safer.

Mind you, this is from a first grader. She had taken on the responsibility of getting everyone to school in the most safe and disciplined manner by consulting a GPS map on her iPad. Frustrated by my ignoring her route sheet corrections, Lucy yelled in my ear, "Mr. Bob, I have told you a thousand times that I do not like going down Grapevine. Turn here and take the other route I gave you."

Me: "Lucy, I cannot do that. I am required to stay on the route given to me."

She sat down in a huff. "Well, it's a dumb route."

Having managed to pass the blame for the dumb route on to the transportation department, (always a great way to solve conflicts) I never heard Lucy mention it again, though I did hear her grumbling under her breath every day we went bouncing happily down the road. Fussbudgets miss a lot of fun stuff.

Losing the re-route order did not prevent Lucy from moving on to other things.

"Mr. Bob, tell Jenny to put her window up, I'm cold." (I wish I could write it in England, English)

"Mr. Bob, tell Jenny to put her window down, I'm hot."

"Mr. Bob, I don't like to walk on the sticky floor. You need to mop it."

It never stopped. I fought the urge to complain. To write her up. Maybe talk to her parents. I chose to not complain, because complaining about a first-grader's complaining was nothing to complain about. I thought about moving her further back in bus, so she was not right in my ear all the time. I nixed that idea. Why should I inflict my problem on innocent children? Plus, forcing her to sit somewhere else would only create problems. All the students had already decided they did not want to be within ten feet of her. They had given her a name, in place of Lucy; they called her Lulu. I managed to stop that behavior on the bus, but I suspect the derogatory use of the name went on, elsewhere.

Because of the persecution that had fallen upon her, because of her choice to be so critical, I decided to put her annoyance aside and give her some acceptance, which she desperately needed. After all, she was just a little girl, trying to grow up, like everyone else. Instead of ignoring her, I decided to engage her in conversation. Something I could easily do since she was always right there leaning over my right shoulder. I asked her simple questions about her day, explained the various workings of the bus, and attempted funny tricks.

I convinced her that I could open the doors by snapping my fingers. It took her a couple days to figure it out. That, while I was snapping my fingers on my right hand, pointed at the doors, I pressed the automatic door button with my left. Or how it was that I could make the porch lights come on at the house at 1500 Jackson every morning, when I turned the corner? Once again by snapping my fingers. Some upper classmate blew the whistle on that one, revealing the existence of motion activated porch lights. The attention, I gave her, did not stop the complaining, but it did offer a bit of relief from its constancy.

One morning, Lucy got on the bus crying, her mother pushing her up the steps and demanding that she calm down. With a baby on a hip and little Tommy by the hand, the mother Townsend turned and walked away. Lucy was silent all the way to school.

The bus driver's manual and the multi-mandates and seminars on sexual harassment and molestation prevent drivers from hugging little girls. (I never liked that rule, born of an age of litigation) However, there is no rule that you cannot hold a crying first-grader's hand. So, when Lucy got on the Panda for the after-school trip home, I took her hand, which was extended over my right shoulder, and asked her what was wrong. She told me. Her little brother, Tommy, was bothering her sleep. Forced to share the same bedroom, she was kept up at all hours of the night by her brother, an overactive child, running around and playing video games. "Mr. Bob, I hate him. Why do I have to sleep in the same room with him?"

For the first time I heard my "Mr. Bob" not followed by some bit of criticism. For the first time I heard Lucy asking for advice rather than giving it. And for the first time, I felt that Lucy and I were having a conversation.

There was not much I could do to solve her problem. All I could do was sympathize with her and let her know that I thought she had a right to complain. I talked to Tommy, as much as you can to a preschooler, about holding it down when his sister was asleep, something I suspect his parents had done a hundred times.

It is possible that Lucy's overblown need to criticize people and to go to lengths of gaining information, beyond the scope of most first graders, were born out significant things happening in her life that were beyond her ability to control. I doubt it was just the loss of bedroom privacy (Maybe not. Everyone needs a place to sleep.). Maybe, it was the move from England. Maybe it was an absent father. Maybe, it was having her only-child world interrupted by these two newcomers. Maybe it was so much attention given to an over-active little brother, whom she hated. Maybe it was the zodiac sign under which she was born. Maybe her DNA. Maybe it was million other things. None of which a bus driver could pin down or seek to resolve. But there is one thing within the control of any bus driver, to decide to hold a hand instead of pushing the problem to the back of the bus.

# Chapter Eight

*Declaring Oneself*

*Tom and Creative Art*

I do not like to use the words "typical high school teenager", because in my experiences on the Panda, high school students do not react well to being identified as typical. If you want to get the stink eye, respond to some a high schooler's behavior with: "Oh, well that's typical".

It is tough being a late-teens teenager struggling with the reality, that in a short while, you will be an independent young adult. Supposedly, out there on your own. It is the "on your own" that creates the typical teenage angst.

Not only is the search for identity tough, physically, socially, and morally, it is scary. So, the oxymoronic occurs. The strong drive to be an induvial is counter-balanced by deep devotion to a group. The contradiction may be obvious, even to a bus driver, but generally, it is not seen by the youth involved. Point out that a student is behaving like a typical teenager by expressing their individuality while at the same time being a bit slavish to a particular group, and you will either get a hostile look or a blank stare that says, "What?".

In the tug-of-war between independence and belonging, going on in the anxious lives of many of my late-teens riders, group identity triumphed over personal identity, most of the time. It was very difficult to get know most students apart from the group they had chosen to join.

There were some country boys and girls in boots and Stetson hats; a few Gothics all in black and silver chains; hipsters with their pants hung low; bow-headed girls with oversized ribbons in their hair; all manner of ethnic dressed Asians and Afro-Americans, lesbian girls in mullet cut, gay boys with an earring on the left. There were geeks and jokes, not necessarily self-exclusive. The scene on the Panda's high school, daily run reminded me of a scene in the movie "Ferris Bueller's Day Off" in which the actress, Edie McClurg, playing the role of Mr. Rooney's (the high school principal) secretary, names the groups of students in the high school who think Ferris is a "righteous dude" "...Motorheads, Potheads, Wasteoids, Dickheads, Sluts, Bloods", etc.

By the time one gets to high school, he or she has already experienced the consequences of not fitting in. Juvenile humankind is neither human nor kind. Kids, like chickens in the barnyard, tend to pick (peck) on the chick less like themselves. No wonder they huddle in groups, just big enough to hide their differences. It is a rare occasion, calling for joy and affirmation, when a young boy or girl stands alone and comes forth with an honest expression of their individuality.

Tom belonged to a group, easily identifiable by the constant presence of a baseball glove, cleats and athletic bag with the high school logo and team insignia. If you were to ask him who he was he would say he was a member of the high school's regional champion baseball team. He will ask you to come see him play in the state tournament, next week. In a short time, you would know what position he played, how hard practice is, why one of his fingers is bent, the score of the last game, and his Texas League fly ball that brought in two runs in the third inning. You would know all of this about his being ball player, but you would not learn a thing about who he was. If you were to ask the stupid question, "No, I mean who are you really?" You would surely get a hostile look or scowl of disbelief. Apart from being a baseball player and a kid who never caused me any grief, I did not know him...until a crisis came into his life.

Tom's mother met me in the high school loading lane one afternoon. Taking me aside, she revealed she and her husband were going through a divorce. Without giving me details, she said I should be aware that she and her boys had a restraining order against him, and I was not to let Tom off the bus if his father was there to pick him up. Her instructions were backed up by a legal document giving me the authority to withhold Tom from his father. Suddenly, I knew something personal about Tom, other than baseball.

For the six years I was lucky to drive the Panda bus, I knew she was an anomaly. Every bus route has a few students who act like jerks. Not the Panda. For six years, it was what I called a "jerk free bus". From time to time there were incidents and accidents, but there was a total absence of jerky behavior, such as sitting backwards, pestering other riders, pester me, talking trash, or dumping trash.

Even in the encounters with Val's anger (See chapter three), I never thought of him as a jerk. On other buses, it was necessary to spell out in detail all the rules of being a good rider. Not so for the Panda crowd. All I had to tell them in the way of rules was spelled out on a bumper sticker pasted above the door...<u>Just Be Nice</u>. It was enough. They were nice kids. Those were good years. As Maj. Frank Burns says in the TV series Mash: "It's nice to be nice to the nice."

So, when I discovered that someone had written on the back of a seat, I was surprised and upset. I thought, maybe some new rider had gotten on my bus, perhaps a friend of one of the regulars. The experience of finding one of your seats written on is upsetting because it is almost impossible to find out who did it. You would think that finding the culprit would be easy, because he or she surely was not able to do it in secret. The seat mate surely knew, as did those who sat across the aisle. But those sources of information were not available to me. No one likes a squealer, especially me. To encourage, by suggestion or by force of intimidation, someone to rat on some other member of the Panda community was not an option, in my book. If defacing a bus seat was a serious crime, I might have been eager to seek out an eyewitness. But it is not. I prefer to believe that it is far more important the perpetrator 'fes up" than be exposed. Besides, someone pointing a finger is immediately open for counter charges. The friends of the fink line up against the defenders of the accused and soon you will need a major law firm to unravel the truth, or worse, parents will get involved.

So, I stopped the bus in a parking lot, pulled the brake, turned off the engine, and stood up. Facing the students, I said, "I would like to know who wrote on the back of seat number eighteen, yesterday. I am not interested in punishing that person, nor will I write them up. I just want that person to have the opportunity to do the responsible thing and own up to it."

I hardly had time to finish the sentence when Tom stood up. "Mr. Bob, I did it. I am sorry. I'll clean it up."

I almost cried. Instead, I went back to Tom and did what the driver's manual says we should not do.

I hugged him, and shaking his hand, I said, "Thank you Tom. That was a brave thing to do." He sat down and we all continued down the road.

Tom did not have to clean up his markings. I did. It was not easy. He had used a black, indelible, ball point pen which etched the ink into the fine Corinthian Naugahyde. Engrossed in my janitorial duty, I had time to wonder why this nice kid had chosen to do this jerky thing. The answer must surely be an acting out of his personal turmoil, involving his parents' divorce. The markings had no wording or pictures to express his feelings, but the slashing lines certainly did.

I did not need to forgive his behavior, because I understood it, and accepted it. Of course, I did not want him to go about expressing his feelings in black ink again, but I did appreciate his courage in standing up...to declare himself amid his friends was a brave act of self-identification.

I stopped scrubbing the marks, as I began to see them as works of original art. Outward expressions of a personal declaration of a young man, who knew that being nice would not cut it. Sometimes, to be real, we are called to do something else then niceness.

The administrators of transportation told me from the first day, that we are part of the whole school system's goals of caring, teaching, and nurturing students. We were all in this together. Of course, a bus driver's ability to be influential in the process of education of any student is handicapped, by the fact that they are not trained as educators, nor do they have the time in a short bus ride to be involved in the life of the students. Therefore, there is a temptation to stick to the business of driving the big yellow beast and ignore opportunities to be a part of the education faculty. But there are teaching moments, when a bus driver as a normal adult human being, can be instructive, and should be.

Tom and the seat-back art offered such a moment for me. I wondered, what other expressions of individual feelings could be hiding in the lives of any of these riders, secreted away in their devotion to memberships groups. Where there other students, like Tom, who would enjoy and gain from expressing their private feelings, writing on the back of a school bus seat? Maybe so. I certainly did not want them drawing on the back of the seats with permanent ink, so I asked the high school art teacher if there was any kind of markers or paint that would stick to vinyl that would be easily removed. She suggested a kind of marker that would fit the bill and gave me a box full, with which I could get started. I was encouraged by her enthusiasm for the project. Making the erasable markers easily available, in the front of the bus, I told the students that they were free to write, draw, or mark up the backs of the seat on the Panda as much as they liked, with the following restrictions. There were to be no organizational, racial, ethnic, religious, or professional sports logos. In short, they were not to express themselves as members of any group. All their art was to be limited to self-expression...personal. Their art was to fit within the fundamental rule of the Panda bus, "*Just Be Nice*". Ugly was okay, but for the sake of my job, no profanity. Regardless of their feelings about someone, either positively or negative, they were to keep their art focus on their personal feeling, free of mentioning any other person or persons.

I am certain, on any other school bus this project would not go well, but I knew these kids. They had being-nice down pat. I trusted they did not need a lot of rules to keep them in bounds.

Judging from the volume of pieces of seat-back art, most of the students participated. For a week, the Panda was an art galery open to not only the high school students doing the work, but also the middle school and elementary riders. Most of the productions were simple markings, phrases, or on the level of stick figures, but some of pieces showed real artistic talent. I toyed with the idea of having the artists identify themselves, but quickly cast it aside. It was best to leave labeling alone.

Unfortunately, I had to terminate the project when things began to get out of control. The younger riders, on my other school routes, were tempted to do their expressions in permanent ink, and some of the high schoolers want to tag the outside of the bus. I was sure that having the Panda bus running around with student art on it would not go well with the goals of Transportation Department. And rightly so. The point of the experiment was to offer an avenue for self-expression, not another way to label the Panda bus as a special group, nor to label its driver a bit weird.

It is no surprise, creative art born of self-expression, shifts so quickly into a desire to create another group. Belonging to a group is comforting. Standing alone requires courage. Something as simple as saying "I did it" announces who you are to everyone around you and is an unusual act of courage and personal identification, not just for late teenagers but everyone. Way to go, Tom.

There is another reason why I do not point out, in a pejorative way, the conflict of expressing one's individuality by donning the symbols of group identity. It would be hypocritical for me to do so. I do the same thing. We all do it. The struggle to express our identity is always in conflict with our need to belong to a group. Solving that tug-of-war is what living is about...making choices. At many points in one's life the decision must be made to either go along, to get along, or risk doing your own thing. The Lovin Spoonful sang it well:

*"Did you ever have to make up your mind?*
*Pick up on one and leave the other behind.*

*It's not often easy and not often kind.*
*Did you ever have to make up your mind?*
*Did you ever have to finally decide?*
*To pick up on one and let the other one ride."*

# Chapter Nine

*Bus Games*

*Fun and Discipline*

As I have mentioned above, my experiences of driving a school bus were uniquely blissful for me and should not be taken a default experience for anyone else. Each driver's experiences are determined by the social environment in which they drive, and no two situations are the same. I was lucky. For most of my years, I was able to establish good repour with 95 % of my students and their parents. I attribute that good fortune to the stability of the middle-class community in which I drove. If I had driven anywhere else, many of the things I did would be dysfunctional for discipline and safety.

With that in mind, I will share with you some things we did on the Panda that were fun, and in some cases against the rules. I do not share these stories as resources for games on anyone else's bus, but to illustrate what can happen where trusting relationships are established.

Another fortunate situation for me and the students on the Panda, was that we had time to get to know and trust one another. After a year of seeing them almost every day of the work week, I got to know their names, and in most cases their parents' names. We had built up many shared events that revealed the nature of each student...events that let me know I could trust them to make their own good decisions, about the boundaries of their behavior.

The Panda bus was brand new when I first drove it. One of its features was a rubber carpet, that ran all the way from the back of the bus to the front, without any connecting joints. The carpet had five grooved tracks extending its full length. I have no idea who, in the back of the bus, thought up the idea placing a marble in one of the grooves and watching it roll frontward whenever the bus stopped and retreat toward the rear when the bus started forward. I thought about stopping the business, but decided to let it go for a while, until it was no longer fascinating to the kid with the marble, and all the other watchers on. The fascination didn't wear off, it grew. Within a few days, I had five marbles rolling up and down the aisle. The students in the back (mostly eighth graders) were placing a marble in each groove. I caught on to the game when I heard them shouting cheers, up and down the bus, "Go! Big Red, Go! Go! Black Beauty, Blue Bell, or Mean Green. I suppose the right thing to do, would be for me to stop the fun. Instead, I put some parameters in place. The games could go on, but the kids in the front seats would need to capture each marble, to keep it from getting under my feet, or down into the stair well. That such a discipline would be assured was based on my years of knowing the kids in the front seats would do it. The rule was enforced by the knowledge that I would stop it if I found any marbles rolling around up front. It never happened. In time the game lost their interest, especially for the underclass boys and girls in the front seats, and everyone went back to doing what they did so well...minding their own business.

There were many such games, we played on the Panda. 1) Five balloons batted back and forth across the aisle, with winners and losers based on the number of balloons counted on the left or right-side team's territory, at any bus stop. The stop defined by when my stop sign went out. The game could continue when the newest kid on board sat down.

No one kept score. It was just fun. 2) Free-for-all, paper wade wars that had no personal targets (Siblings, and boy/girlfriends sometimes ignored that rule.) Everyone against everyone. The driver was declared a non-combatant, as was any student who took a vow of pacifism (There were a few). Paper wad games were played on the afternoon runs, of the last day of each semester, because the students had plenty of paper to wade up, from the material returned to them, by their teachers. 3) Peanut wars (canceled). Sometimes, when playing, mistakes are made. I made a big one allowing a peanut war to break out. I completely forgot that some youths are allergic to peanuts. I apologized to the kids for allowing this game to go on. I was lucky that no one was damaged. 4) Learning from the peanut mistake, I did not stop various other varieties of warfare, small wet sponges, water pistols, and small nerf balls (I had to stop that one. It is amazing how hard a high school student can throw a nerf ball). There were rules of course to control the excesses. No standing up was allowed in any of the games unless I stopped the bus and allowed the war to go for a while.

I mention these games because it is in such playfulness that bonding occurs. I know that such behavior would be totally out of place on most bus routes, but some form of playfulness can be experienced on any bus. For example, I did not allow the games, mentioned above, to be played on an elementary route. Children, aged below the 5th grade, are not mature enough to know when to stop. However, there were games I played with them, almost every day. Most of them having to do with Peep-a-Boo in the rear-view mirror or getting them to draw pictures on construction paper. The cover of this book is from one of hundred given to me, over the years. I discovered that I could get little panda bears on Amazon that had magnets on them. I handed them out and the kids would plaster them up all over the bus. Some child discovered you could stick the pandas' magnets together and make a panda string. With little red bows around their necks the panda strings made excellent Christmas garland and Chinese New Year's streamers.

Driving a school bus without having any fun is like being up to bat and never swinging.

# Epilogue

In the United States, 300,000 school buses carry 25 million students to and from school each day. Those students are seventy time more likely to get to school safely on a school bus, than traveling in a car, according to the National Highway Traffic Safety Administration.

As a novice driver that was a bit sobering to know, because I was not confident that I could drive a big yellow bus, without running into something or avoid someone hitting me, that would screw up the NHTSA statistics. The jitters increase, when you know you are about to haul the most precious cargo in the world...children. Our next generation depends on you getting those loads safe and sound, to and from school and on field trips to only heaven and GPS knows were.

The four-lane highway, I was attempting to enter, with forty-five high schoolers on board, was bumper to bumper. I waited the mandatory count of 10 cars, my father had taught me was a fair number to allow to pass, before darting into whatever space may be there. Not only is entering on-coming traffic, based on number counts, a foolish idea, trying it with a school bus is insanity. Ignoring my father's example, and holding true to what my trainer taught me, I waited and waited, until I thought I had a safe space. School buses are not sports cars. They are not so fast, nor so small. I miss judged the space, and found a guy riding on my back bumper, blowing his horn. As he roared pass, he leaned over in his seat and shot me a finger. For a second, I thought about honking back and returning the sentiment, while shouting, "Yeah! You too buddy!" Being the mature human being, I am, and in respect to everyone on board, I just mumbled a vulgarity under my breath.

When I got back to base, I found a note in my box, requesting I see my supervisor. I knew why. The single finger guy had seen the phone number on the Panda's rear bumper and called in to report my recklessness. So, with anxiety and my eyes on the floor, I went to receive my reprimand and a couple demerits.

Things were made worse for me because the sup's office had no door. My moment of humiliation and poor driving skills would soon be known to the whole world.

The boss welcomed me with a kind, "Hi Bob, how are you doing?"

Somewhat thrown off by his geniality, I responded, "Fine, and you?

"Great. Have a seat." He spoke. So, I sat down. He came around from behind his desk and sat down in front of me, with our knees nearly touching. Too much time has passed for me to remember exactly what he said, but I know he showed interest in how my transition from being a pastor to driving a school bus was going. I related, that other than just learning how to operate a big bus, things were going well. I had a great deal of experience in human relations, as a pastor, so that part of the job was not much different. He shared some stories of accidents, he had during his early years of driving. He joked, "Maybe that is why I am sitting behind a desk and not out there behind the wheel." Our banter continued for a while. In a pause, I got up to leave, having forgotten the reason I had been summoned there.

As I stood, he said, "You know a teacher called in this morning and said you had cut him off."

"I suspected, he might", I said timidly.

"Well, watch that kind of thing. Safety is more important than getting to school on time." (I thought about finding out who the teacher was, who shot me the finger and reporting him to his principal. Deciding that would open a bag of worms, I let it drop.)

I found out, at the end of the semester, I had gotten a demerit for the infraction.

The boss in this story, and most other supervisors and administrators under whom I served, all showed the same style of leadership. They took the time and presence, necessary to get to know their subordinates. Relationships were built. Procedures for enforcing the rules and assigning consequences were turn from being methods for assuring good behavior into opportunities to learn and grow into becoming better drivers, in a supportive community. The fundamental talent of those supervisors was the ability to walk gracefully on the edge of judging, without being judgmental, of being a boss without being bossy.

It is a rare talent, that depends on one's ability to establish trusting relationships, which in turn takes time. Unfortunately, in many fast-growing urban school districts changes happen with such urgency, there is not enough time to get to know people.

I drove a school bus for two years in the small town of Schulenburg, Texas. I had no manual of directions, or written list of rules to follow. All I was given was a route sheet and keys to a bus. There was no system of demerits. No need for one. Everything was based on trustworthiness. I was trusted, because my supervisor was also my kid's principal and a member of my congregation. He knew me...as did about everyone in the town. When I took out a farmer's mailbox, the farmer casually mentioned it to my director friend, over a beer in a deer blind. "That darn preacher you hired knocked over my mailbox." I got no demerits. My punishment was a Saturday morning, planting and painting a new mailbox. Which I had to pay for. Much of the trust, placed in me, was based on the knowledge, if I did something wrong, you could trust that someone knew about, and it would be the topic of conversation all over town. I knew, if I continued nailing mailboxes, I would continue spending

Saturday mornings on the farm, and be reminded of it by some parishioner, on Sunday morning.

Order, based on trusting one another, is ease in stable, small town transportation departments, but not so much, in rapidly changing urban settings. It is sad but true.

After being taken off my precious Panda route, I was given a new route, with all new riders. Children who did not know me, nor did I know them. One morning as students were unloading a middle school, a kid decided he would dispense with the safe way off the bus and jump from the top landing. "Hey, kid", I yelled at him. "Come back here and go down the steps the way I told you." With a defiant look, he went back. to the top of the stairs. After stomping down every one of them, he turned to me and said, "There. You happy?" I believe I would have written him up for the disrespect, if I had not caught myself thinking, "What was I thinking?" Where did the disrespect begin? It began in my yelling at him. It began when I called him "kid", because I had not taken the time (or had the time) to know his name. I began when I said, I had told him to use all the steps. I had not done that.

That afternoon, when he got on the bus, I went back to him and told him I was sorry, I had embarrassed him by yelling at him. I asked him his name. He told me his name was, Jack. I said, "Hi Jack, I'm Mr. Bob". A big chunk of the reason I apologized to Jack, was because I was wrong. But a secondary and very important reason, was I did not want an angry teen-age boy sitting, mostly out of view, behind my back. Believe me, if you want to have order on your bus, you need as many friends as you can sitting behind you. One angry student can ruin your day, or your whole year.

Thus, began the on-going task of friendship building on a new route for bus #132...and again the next semester.

Something is getting lost in the big, fast, and new. What is getting lost is time. Time to get to know whom and what to trust, in today's world. The Panda is a parable... and a prophesy.

My great admiration goes to the professional men and women serving in rapidly growing and ever-changing urban school districts (Rural, too), responsible for running well ordered, safe, and dependable student transportation, while taking time to build working relationships of trust and good morale.

# Acknowledgments

If my eighty-three-year-old brain could fully function, I could rattle off the names of all the people who have had a hand in my writing this book. Alas, their names are gone, and I do not know where to find them. For example, somewhere out there, is a former parishioner of mine, who was a superintendent of Taylor ISD. He mentored me through my path to faculty certification in the William Glaser Institute. I thank him and the Institute.

Formative to my soul, the faculty members of Perkins Theological Seminary-SMU are too many to name or remember. They opened my eyes to the power of myth and the parables of Jesus...and Jesus.

How about the United Methodist Church and forty years of parishioners egging me on?

More recently, the Round Rock ISD Transportation Department and everyone around it.

I was (and still am) greatly blessed by being a tiny part of the lives of thousands of children and youth who rode the Panda. Thank heavens for my bosses, Dennis Bigbee, Joan Sutton, and Vicky Rowald, whose leadership provided nonjudgmental judgments and friendship. I thank all those fellow bus drivers, who shared their stories. I still treasure the friendships of my bus driver buddies, Jim O'Connor, Don Morton, Keith Young, and the late Dwaine Palmer. We were a great team.

I cannot say enough good stuff, about my editor, Richard Hacker. Back in the 80s, he was my associate pastor at Westlake UMC, Austin. From there he turned his vocation toward being a novelist. (I assume it was not my senior pastoring that drove the decision) He made the right choice. He has written several, award winning, novels, such as *Kilt Dead and Worse, Die Back,* and *The Bifurcation of Dungsten Crease,* to name a few. When I was looking around for an editor, my friend The Rev. Sid Hall, former pastor of Trinity Church, Austin, reminded me of Richard, who had helped him edit one of his books. Richard accepted my request for editorship and then stuck me with the exorbitant fee of two beers and a breakfast taco. No matter the cost, this book would have never made it to publication, without the technical support and wise counsel of Richard Hacker.

The Rev. John McFarland and his good wife, Helen came cheaper. It was one of John's books, *The Strange Calling,* (a collection of fascinating, parish ministry, stories) that became the model for my book of stories. More directly, their experience and kind corrections kept me focused, saying things like, "Just stick to telling the stories, that is what you are good at." So far, I have not received a bill from them...though I owe them a fortune.

And thank you, Vicky Rowald and my wife, Marilyn for going the second mile in proofreading my work. It was badly needed.

Finally, I thank the members of my family. My next oldest brother, Jim, and his wife Jody Coulter-Parsons were some of the first people I reached out to read my stories and offer opinions. Jim has published a couple books including, *Hillary Clinton and Other Bullies.* I figured if he could write a book, so could I. Jody wrote a popular Arkansas history book, *Back Yonder.* Early on, she showed some of my stories to her teacher friends, and they loved them, and encouraged me to publish. My oldest brother, Joe said I told good stories, but my grammar, spelling, sentence structure, and composition were poor, but I should not let little things like that stop me. I thank my long deceased, Aunt Clara Walker-Hartsfield, who taught English composition and grammar at Tech High School in San Antonio, years ago. When I was a boy, I would write her letters and she would send them back to me with G.I.s (Gross Illiteracies) and red ink marks all over them. I thank my parents, Joe, and Lillian, who with great sacrifice and good example, pushed me to get a good education and a be a decent human being. Most of all, I thank my loving wife of fifty-nine years, Marilyn, for her patient support of this writing addiction I have.

# About the Author

After serving forty years as a United Methodist pastor in Indiana and Texas, Bob Parsons drove a school bus for fifteen years. He is a graduate of Indiana University, and Perkins School of Theology, SMU; was a faculty member of the William Glasser Institute, and a president of Texas PFLAG. He and his wife, Marilyn live in Pflugerville, Texas. When Bob is not having a beer with his bus driver buddies, you might find him fishing for reds and trout on the Texas coast, relaxing with a bourbon and water and smoking a cigar on the back porch, or taking a nap.

You can find Bob on Facebook at http://www.facebook.com/BPar410

The Panda Bus